21st Century Skills **INNOVATION** *Library*

Emergency Care

by Susan H. Gray

INNOVATION IN   MEDICINE

Published in the United States of America by Cherry Lake Publishing
Ann Arbor, Michigan
www.cherrylakepublishing.com

Content Adviser: Noshene Ranjbar, MD

Design: The Design Lab

Photo Credits: Cover and page 3, ©Jochen Tack/Alamy; page 4, ©Pete Klinger, used under license from Shutterstock, Inc.; page 6, ©AP Photo/Mathew B. Brady; page 8, ©Mary Evans Picture Library/Alamy; page 10, ©The Print Collector/Alamy; page 12, ©Juriah Mosin, used under license from Shutterstock, Inc.; page 15, ©aceshot1, used under license from Shutterstock, Inc.; page 16, ©Tyler Hartl, used under license from Shutterstock, Inc.; page 19, ©prism_68, used under license from Shutterstock, Inc.; page 20, ©The Stock Asylum, LLC/Alamy; page 21, ©AP Photo/M. Spencer Green; page 23, ©John Sartin, used under license from Shutterstock, Inc.; page 24, ©Kadak, used under license from Shutterstock, Inc.; page 25, ©Lucian Coman, used under license from Shutterstock, Inc.; page 26, ©AP Photo; page 27, ©Richard Sheppard/Alamy; page 28, ©AP Photo/Racine Journal-Times, Mark Hertzberg

Library of Congress Cataloging-in-Publication Data
Gray, Susan H., 1954–
 Emergency care / by Susan H. Gray.
   p. cm.–(Innovation in medicine)
 ISBN-13: 978-1-60279-230-2
 ISBN-10: 1-60279-230-5
 1. Emergency medical services–Juvenile literature. 2. Medical innovations–Juvenile literature. I. Title. II. Series.
 RA645.5.G73 2009
 362.18–dc22   2008014181

*Cherry Lake Publishing would like to acknowledge the work of
The Partnership for 21st Century Skills.
Please visit www.21stcenturyskills.org for more information.*

CONTENTS

Chapter One
**From Chariots to Flying
Ambulances**   **4**

Chapter Two
Turning Things Around   **12**

Chapter Three
More Changes   **16**

Chapter Four
**The Future of Emergency
Medicine**   **20**

Chapter Five
Famous Innovators   **23**

Glossary   30
For More Information   31
Index   32
About the Author   32

CHAPTER ONE

From Chariots to Flying Ambulances

Today's ambulances usually arrive quickly to transport sick or injured people to the hospital.

"Joe, look out for that rock!" shouted Mario.

Mario's warning call was a second too late. Joe hit the rock and flew over his bike's handlebars. Mario jumped off his bike and raced over to his friend who was lying on the ground holding his arm.

"Ouch!" yelped Joe as Mario touched his arm. "Please don't touch it. It hurts so much."

"I think you broke it. We'd better call 911. You're bleeding, too!"

Mario took out his cell phone and dialed 911 for emergency help.

"Hang on, Joe!" said Mario as he finished giving the dispatcher the information about the accident. "Help will be here soon."

Just then they heard the sound of an ambulance siren getting closer. Soon, an ambulance pulled up and an emergency medical technician (EMT) jumped out.

"Looks like you took quite a fall. Don't worry! We'll get you to the hospital in no time."

Most people are familiar with the sound of an ambulance siren. The siren tells everyone that an ambulance crew is hurrying to help someone who needs medical care.

Emergency medical help has not always been so quick or efficient. In ancient Rome, gladiators often battled fierce animals or each other to entertain crowds. These men ended up with broken bones, deep stab wounds, and torn limbs. A chariot came to move their broken bodies out of the way. Then it was off to a doctor who could do little to help them.

This was the primitive state of emergency medicine for centuries. Even the *idea* of good, quick medical care did not exist.

In the 1500s, doctors began taking small steps to change things. Those who performed **amputations** began using a device to stop the bleeding. The device was called a **tourniquet**. It was usually a strip of cloth or leather that was tied tightly above the spot where the limb had been cut off. In 1674, military doctors began using the tourniquet on battlefields. It allowed them to slow or stop even the most severe bleeding from arms and legs. This often kept soldiers from dying of blood loss on the field.

Wounded soldiers wait for medical attention during the American Civil War. Treating patients in the battlefield led to many advances in general emergency care.

Many lost their lives, however, waiting to be carried to the doctor. Military surgeons usually worked in tents or buildings some distance from the battlefield. Wounded soldiers either were left to die or were lugged by comrades to the surgeon's tent.

This pitiful treatment of soldiers troubled Dr. Dominique Jean Larrey. Larrey was a French army surgeon in the 1790s. He believed that injured soldiers suffered too much while lying on the field. He designed a horse-drawn carriage that could transport a medical team out to the wounded. It would then bring injured soldiers to safety. Larrey called his vehicle the *ambulance volante*, or flying ambulance.

Larrey also came up with the idea of **triage**. This is the practice of separating patients into groups and treating them according to the seriousness of their injuries. Before triage, officers with minor wounds received help first, while lower-ranking men with serious injuries waited.

In the American Civil War (1861–1865), the need for emergency medical care was great. Even in small battles, hundreds of soldiers could be wounded. Sometimes, the musicians in the army's band hauled these men to the field hospital. Occasionally, ambulance wagons did this job. These wagons were heavy, covered wooden carts. They were sometimes so uncomfortable and jarring that the injured men begged to be let out. Some ambulances carried medicines for the wounded. Unfortunately, the drivers often kept these medicines for themselves. While America was recovering from the Civil War, two military officers in England were working on a new idea. The two men were Dr. Peter Shepherd and Colonel Francis Duncan. They knew that sometimes people died because they did not receive even

Learning how to bandage a head wound was part of early first aid courses. Here a man wraps the head of a young rider who has fallen from his horse.

the simplest medical care or did not receive it quickly enough. They decided that ordinary citizens should learn to handle small medical emergencies.

In 1878, they developed a course in first aid and began teaching the public. Their classes became very popular. People were pleased to know how to deal with everyday emergencies. Students in these classes learned how to properly bandage head injuries, how to stop serious bleeding, and how to help someone who had fainted. Classes met in a church in Woolwich, England.

Not long after the courses began, tragedy hit the town of Woolwich. A storage building collapsed, burying 160 workers. A large-scale rescue began, and many townspeople applied their first-aid training. A few months later, a pleasure boat on the nearby river was rammed by another craft and began to sink. As victims were brought ashore, the townsfolk again used their training to help. Shepherd and Duncan's classes had proven very valuable.

About this same time, Clara Barton of the United States visited Europe. Barton had witnessed the suffering of the Civil War and had often provided medical supplies for the military. In Europe, she learned of the International Red Cross—an organization that helped wounded soldiers in several countries. Barton wanted to set up a similar organization in the United States.

Clara Barton founded the American Red Cross in 1881. This agency has branch organizations around the world.

In 1881, she and her friends started the American Red Cross. Its mission was to assist American soldiers and their families. During World War I (1914–1918) and World War II (1939–1945), membership grew rapidly. Adults gathered medical supplies for the soldiers, and children donated their pennies to the Junior Red Cross. The organization also began "blood drives" for the wounded.

Slowly, the care of injured soldiers improved. First aid was becoming more and more popular with the public.

The idea of emergency medicine was just beginning to take shape.

Hospitals, however, were slow to catch on. In the first half of the 20th century, few hospitals had emergency departments. Those that did were poorly equipped and poorly staffed. Patients who had been in accidents rode to the hospital in the back of a **hearse**. Once they arrived, they were treated by an attendant with no emergency training.

In 1966, a branch of the United States government published a shocking report on accidents and emergency care. It said that almost 50,000 people had died in car wrecks in the last year, and the number was going up. It also said that many hospital emergency departments were outdated. Another problem was that too many emergency workers were poorly trained. People had ignored this growing problem, the report said, and it was time for a change.

Learning & Innovation Skills

When Clara Barton started the American Red Cross, the group's aim was to help soldiers and their families. Over time, its mission grew to include nurses' training, health education programs, and help for people in disaster areas.

After hurricanes Rita and Katrina hit the southern United States in 2005, the Red Cross provided shelter and meals to thousands of victims. Have you ever seen the Red Cross in action? What do you think would happen during disasters if organizations such as the Red Cross didn't exist?

CHAPTER TWO

Turning Things Around

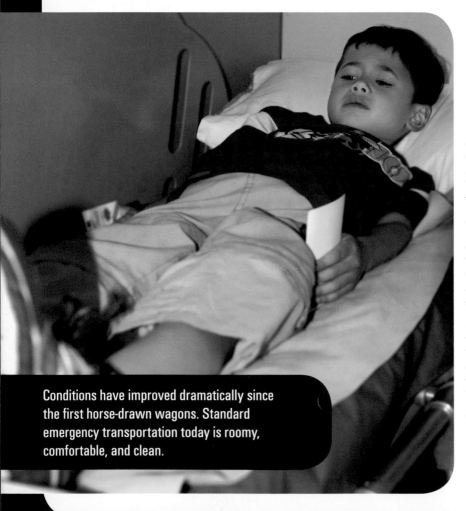

Conditions have improved dramatically since the first horse-drawn wagons. Standard emergency transportation today is roomy, comfortable, and clean.

Change came slowly at first. Even in the 1960s, hearses from local funeral homes were being used to transport injured people. Those who drove them or who loaded patients had no medical training. In some cases, they probably harmed the patients more than they helped.

Worse still, patients who made it to the hospital were in for an unpleasant surprise. Emergency rooms could be filled with people who had minor injuries, had too much alcohol to drink, or were just lonely. Hospital staff had little emergency training and few pieces of equipment to work with. The only doctor available might be an eye or ear specialist—not someone who could handle an auto accident or heart attack victim.

The military used many advanced emergency techniques, but few people believed these could be used in **civilian** hospitals. In the 1950s, Dr. J. D. Farrington disagreed. Farrington saw that military doctors had learned a lot by treating soldiers in war. It seemed to him that all their knowledge was going to waste in peacetime. Instead, it could be applied to everyday emergencies and accidents.

Farrington began working with other doctors on this problem. First, they decided, ambulance staff should be better trained. So they began teaching classes. Over time, the classes included training on handling more and more

Learning & Innovation Skills

Many innovations in emergency medicine come from the military. This is because doctors in wartime must deal with many terrible injuries, and they must handle them quickly. Today, some military doctors are using a special bandage on injured soldiers. It is coated with a substance that causes wounds to stop bleeding almost immediately. Do you think these bandages would be useful in civilian hospitals? Why or why not?

kinds of emergencies. The staff became better prepared to face them.

In 1966, the U.S. government became involved. In that year, lawmakers passed the National Highway Safety Act. Among other things, it listed the pieces of equipment that should be in ambulances. It also laid out the kind of training that ambulance staff should have. Ambulance services were finally improving, but hospital emergency rooms were as poor as ever.

John Wiegenstein, a young doctor in Michigan, realized that things could be better. One day, he was working in the emergency room. Suddenly, a nurse rushed in and said a man had brought in his child who was suffocating. Something was blocking the child's airway. Wiegenstein quickly cut a hole in his patient's throat, and the child began breathing. The young doctor had never done this type of surgery before. It made him see how poorly prepared he was for an emergency. He worried that many other people might die simply because their emergency doctors did not know what to do for them. Wiegenstein began talking to others about this.

In 1968, he gathered a small group of doctors who had the same concerns. They called themselves the American College of Emergency Physicians. They decided that doctors who worked in emergency departments should have special training. They should learn how to handle all sorts of emergencies—heavy bleeding, heart attacks, severe burns, and other life-threatening problems.

It took years to get other doctors to accept this. Some thought that emergency doctors might "steal their patients." Others did not realize just how poorly prepared most emergency doctors were. But they could not ignore the facts for long. More patients needed emergency care, and more were dying because they couldn't get it. Slowly, everyone realized there should be doctors who specialized in emergencies. At last, things were changing.

Most large, modern hospitals now employ specially trained doctors and nurses to staff their emergency rooms.

CHAPTER THREE

More Changes

To call for emergency care anywhere in the United States, dial 911.

Once people grasped the idea of emergency medicine, innovations came quickly. Some have improved the ambulance systems, and others have affected hospitals.

Lawmakers have had a hand in this. For one thing, they decided that 911 should be the emergency telephone number everywhere in the country. They also decided that emergency medical technicians (EMTs) should take classes and learn how to handle many different types of emergencies. Ambulances should have better designs and include plenty of room for equipment, the EMTs, and patients.

The new laws were great, but issues still came up. Ambulances couldn't go everywhere. How could they reach emergencies in wilderness areas? How could they go where there were no roads? Had the military dealt with this issue?

The armed forces had already solved this problem by using helicopters. These aircraft need only a small landing area. They could be adapted to hold emergency equipment, EMTs, and patients. In 1972, a hospital in Denver, Colorado, became the first to try using helicopters.

New hospital equipment came into use, too. The **defibrillator** was one such item. Doctors knew that **fibrillation** in the bottom part of the heart caused many deaths. In fibrillation, the bottom part of the heart flutters rapidly instead of beating normally. While it flutters, it cannot pump blood out to the rest of the patient's body. The longer this continues, the more likely a patient is to die.

Doctors and engineers came together to see what could be done for such patients. They came up with a large machine that could shock the heart into beating

21st Century Content

 In England, the government heads up the National Defibrillator Programme. This is an effort to place defibrillators in busy places, such as airports and train stations, all over the country. It is the first program of its kind in the world and has saved many lives. Workers in England have even helped other European countries start their own programs.

normally. Because the machine stopped fibrillations, it was called a defibrillator.

The defibrillator could save lives—as long as the patients were in the hospital when they needed it. This was not good enough for Dr. Frank Pantridge. Pantridge was a heart doctor in Ireland. He thought that ambulance crews should also have defibrillators. In order for this to happen, he knew the defibrillators would have to be small and portable. Pantridge asked technicians to help him develop such a machine. They created several different models before finally producing a small defibrillator that could be carried in one hand.

One of the greatest innovations in emergency medicine is not a piece of equipment; it's a procedure. **Cardiopulmonary resuscitation** (CPR) is a way to save someone whose heartbeat and breathing have stopped.

CPR is a combination of two other procedures—mouth-to-mouth resuscitation and cardiac massage. Mouth-to-mouth resuscitation was developed in the

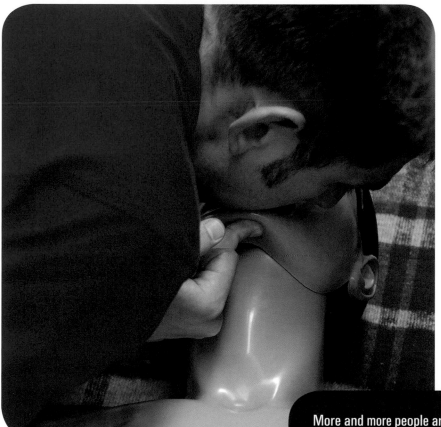

More and more people are learning how to perform CPR and basic first aid. Knowing CPR and first aid can save lives.

1950s to revive people who had stopped breathing. It often helped people who had nearly drowned. An electrical engineer developed cardiac massage. It was a method of pushing a patient's chest to force blood through a stopped heart. In 1960, Dr. Peter Safar put the two methods together. Since its creation, CPR has saved countless lives.

CHAPTER FOUR

The Future of Emergency Medicine

A hospital blood bank stores packages of different blood types.

Today, scientists are still working on better and faster ways to handle emergencies. Some are trying to develop "artificial blood." After disasters occur, blood banks often run low. Not enough people donate blood to meet the need. So scientists are trying to create a blood substitute.

Scientists and engineers are working on developing artificial blood. Here a lab technician works on making a blood substitute in Evanston, Illinois.

The substitute would contain molecules that carry oxygen all over the body, just as real blood does. It would also be easier to store and would not carry any disease. EMTs could give this blood to accident victims to help keep them alive until they reached a hospital.

In 2007, scientists introduced a new type of patch to place on patients. The patch can "read" the patient's blood. It can tell whether the blood has the right balance of chemicals in it. Such a patch might come in handy for emergency workers. It would keep them from having to draw blood and send it to a lab for these readings.

In some rural areas, emergency teams are trying out television cameras to help them work on patients. The cameras send pictures of the patient to doctors at distant hospitals. The doctors decide what the patient needs, and the rural team carries out their orders. The camera allows emergency doctors to help patients who are far away. Perhaps this equipment will be used more in the future.

Doctors, nurses, and EMTs are now learning to handle disasters. Hurricanes, collapsed bridges, and other wide-scale **catastrophes** call for speedy, level-headed responses. Medical teams are practicing now for future events. They are learning to triage more quickly and how to decide whom to call if they need more help.

CHAPTER FIVE

Famous Innovators

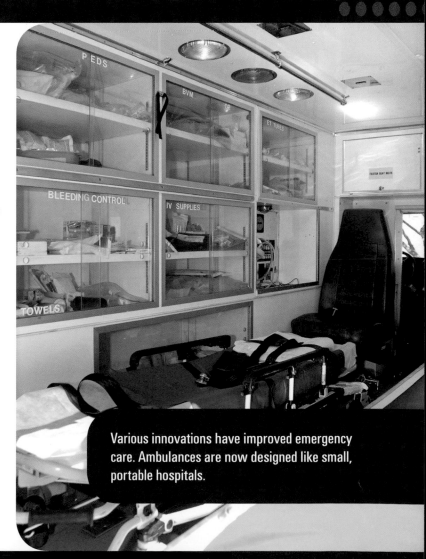

Various innovations have improved emergency care. Ambulances are now designed like small, portable hospitals.

What does it take to be an innovator? Looking at the lives of people who have successfully put new ideas into practice can give you some clues.

Dominique Jean Larrey

Dr. Dominique Jean Larrey was an innovator whose influence is still felt today. Larrey was born in 1766. As a young man, he received medical training from his uncle who was a doctor. While serving as a doctor in the French army, Larrey was saddened at how slowly the wounded soldiers received care. With no speedy transport to field hospitals, the injured would lie on the battlefield until fighting ended and help arrived. He thought the soldiers deserved better. That's what moved him to develop his ambulance volante.

Larrey parked his flying ambulance as close to the line of battle as possible. From there, the vehicle rushed off to wounded soldiers. Medical attendants quickly hoisted the men inside and hauled them to the

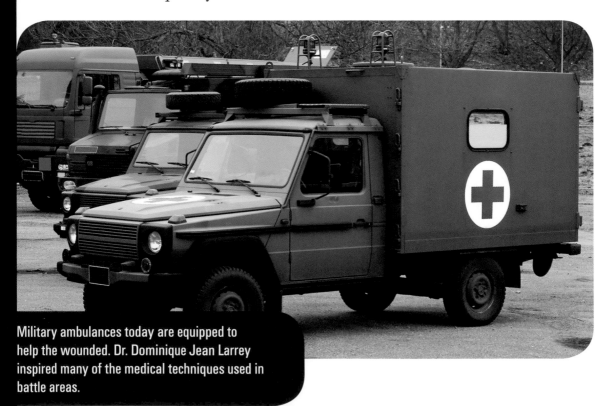

Military ambulances today are equipped to help the wounded. Dr. Dominique Jean Larrey inspired many of the medical techniques used in battle areas.

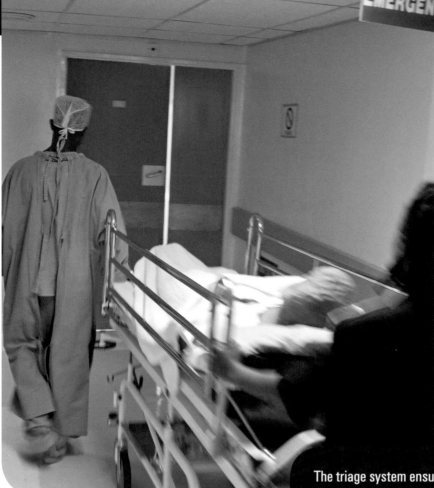

field hospital. There Larrey saw that they were triaged appropriately. "Those who are dangerously wounded should receive the first attention, without regard to rank or distinction," he wrote.

Today, ambulances still bring trained medical workers to injured people. Hospitals still use the triage system for sorting patients. In honor of his innovations, Larrey is often called the Father of Emergency Medicine.

Dr. Charles Drew discovered a way to preserve blood for emergencies. He was the first African American examiner on the American Board of Surgery.

Charles Drew

Many people owe their lives to Dr. Charles Drew. Drew taught biology in high school before studying medicine. By the time he completed medical school in 1933, he was already interested in blood **transfusions**. He knew that they saved lives but also that they presented problems.

Donated blood **deteriorated** quickly. It would last only a few days before needing to be thrown out. Drew thought it was shameful that such a lifesaver was so often discarded. He began studying blood in detail. Eventually, he developed a way to preserve blood for longer periods

This statue commemorates the life and work of the innovative doctor Frank Pantridge. He invented the portable defibrillator to help patients who can't get to a hospital quickly.

of time. Drew's innovation has made it possible for blood to be stored and shipped to disaster areas all over the world. It was a great discovery for emergency medicine.

Frank Pantridge

Dr. Frank Pantridge was another innovator. He saw many patients who needed emergency care for their heart problems but who could not get help in time. He decided to do something about it.

At the time, hospitals had defibrillators to correct the fluttering heart. These were large machines and needed electricity from the hospital's supply to work. Pantridge figured that if most people suffering from fibrillation were outside the hospital, then defibrillators needed to be outside the hospital, too. He started working on a portable unit.

A country sheriff displays a portable defibrillator for use on cardiac arrest victims.

The first portable defibrillator was huge. It weighed 154 pounds (70 kilograms) and got its electricity from car batteries. Pantridge did not stop with this model, though. In the 1960s, he came up with a small defibrillator that weighed only 6.6 pounds (3 kg). These handheld defibrillators have since saved many lives. They can now be found in airports, subway stations, and even shopping centers around the world, where trained people can easily get to them.

Emergency medicine has come a long way from the time of gladiators and chariots. Every year, new equipment and techniques make emergency care even better than before.

Life & Career Skills

Not all medical innovators are doctors. William Kouwenhoven, an electrical engineer, is one example. Kouwenhoven was interested in the electrical signals that cause the heart to beat. In particular, he wondered how to fix those signals when a heart was beating abnormally. He led a team of people who invented the defibrillator. He also developed cardiac massage. He was able to take what he knew about electricity and apply it to the field of medicine.

Glossary

amputations (am-pyoo-TAY-shunz) operations in which a limb is removed from the body

cardiopulmonary (kar-dee-o-PULL-muh-nehr-ee) having to do with the heart and the lungs

catastrophes (kuh-TASS-truh-feez) great disasters or tragedies

civilian (sih-VILL-yun) having to do with nonmilitary things

defibrillator (dee-FIB-rih-lay-tur) a machine that shocks a fluttering (or fibrillating) heart to force it to return to a normal beat

deteriorated (dee-TIR-ee-ur-ay-ted) went bad

fibrillation (fib-rih-LAY-shun) uncontrolled fluttering or quivering

hearse (HURSS) a large car from a funeral home that is used to transport the bodies of dead people

resuscitation (rih-suss-suh-TAY-shun) the act of reviving someone

tourniquet (TUR-nih-kut) a strip of cloth, rubber, or leather that is tightened around a limb to stop heavy bleeding

transfusions (tranz-FYOO-zhunz) the act of transferring blood or another liquid into the blood vessels of a person

triage (TREE-ahzh) the practice of separating patients into groups based on the seriousness of their injuries

For More Information

BOOKS

Kalman, Bobbie. *Hospital Workers in the Emergency Room*. New York: Crabtree Publishing Company, 2004.

Levine, Michelle. *Ambulances*. Minneapolis: Lerner Publications, 2004.

Marsh, Carole. *Li, the Excellent EMT!* Peachtree City, GA: Gallopade International, 2003.

Townsend, John. *Bedpans, Blood and Bandages: A History of Hospitals*. Austin, TX: Raintree, 2006.

WEB SITES

KidsHealth: What Happens in the Emergency Room?
www.kidshealth.org/kid/feel_better/places/er.html
Find out what to expect if you visit the emergency room

Medicine in the Civil War
www.nps.gov/archive/gett/gettkidz/doctor.htm
Learn more about the practice of medicine during the American Civil War

Medline Plus: Children's Page
www.nlm.nih.gov/medlineplus/childrenspage.html
Links to all sorts of medical information, including emergency medicine

Index

911 emergency number, 4, 16–17

ambulances, 5, 7–8, 13, 14, 16, 17, 18, 24–25
ambulance volante, 7, 24–25
ambulance wagons, 7–8
American College of Emergency Physicians, 14–15
American Red Cross, 10, 11
amputations, 5–6
armed forces. *See* military.
"artificial blood," 20–21

bandages, 13
Barton, Clara, 9–10, 11
blood banks, 20, 26–27
blood drives, 10, 20
blood test patches, 22
blood transfusions, 26

cameras, 22

cardiac massage, 18, 19, 29
cardiopulmonary resuscitation (CPR), 18–19
catastrophes. *See* disasters.
Civil War, 7–8, 9

defibrillators, 17–18, 28–29
disasters, 11, 20, 22
dispatchers, 4–5
Drew, Charles, 26–27
Duncan, Francis, 8–9

education, 9, 11, 13–14, 17
emergency doctors, 14–15, 22
emergency medical technicians (EMTs), 5, 17, 21, 22, 25
emergency rooms, 11, 13, 14

Farrington, J. D., 13
fibrillation, 17–18, 28

field hospitals, 7, 25
first aid, 9, 10

gladiators, 5, 29

hearses, 11, 12
helicopters, 17
history, 5–11, 12–15, 16–19
hurricanes, 11, 22

International Red Cross, 9

Junior Red Cross, 10

Kouwenhoven, William, 29

Larrey, Dominique Jean, 7, 23–25
laws, 14, 16–17

medicines, 8
military, 6, 7–8, 9, 10, 13, 17, 24–25
mouth-to-mouth resuscitation, 18–19

National Defibrillator Programme, 18
National Highway Safety Act, 14

Pantridge, Frank, 18, 27–29
portable defibrillators, 18, 28–29

Red Cross. *See* American Red Cross; International Red Cross.
rural areas, 22

Safar, Peter, 19
Shepherd, Peter, 8–9

tourniquet, 6
triage, 7, 22, 25

Wiegenstein, John, 14
World War I, 10
World War II, 10

About the Author

Susan H. Gray has a master's degree in zoology. She has taught college-level courses in biology, anatomy, and physiology. She also has written more than 90 science and reference books for children. In her free time, she likes to garden and play the piano. Susan lives in Cabot, Arkansas, with her husband, Michael, and many pets.